Diary Of The Heart

Little Red Book

W. R. Watkins

'Diary Of The Heart: Little Red Book'
Written by W. R. Watkins
Edited by W. R. Watkins

Copyright © 2015, W. R. Watkins

First published in paperback 2015
First published in hardback 2016

Connect with the author
Facebook: facebook.com/AuthorWRWatkins
Twitter: @WRWATKINS2014
Instagram: @wrwatkinsofficial
Tumblr: wrwatkinsofficial.tumblr.com
GoodReads: goodreads.com/WRWatkins
Official Website: wrwatkins.wix.com/wrwatkinsofficial

3rd Edition, 2016.

Cover art designed by W. R. Watkins

This is dedicated to

....,

this is for you.

Dear Reader,

Thank you so, so much for buying my third poetry book, and the second in the *Diary Of The Heart* series. I will keep on saying this, but it does mean a lot to me, and it drives me to continue producing (what I hope is) good quality material, that you will enjoy.

Writing the material for this book, felt so different compared to *An Obsessive Infatuation*. Whilst I enjoyed writing the poems for *An Obsessive Infatuation*, there were times where I felt that some of the material was forced and less authentic.

By 'authentic,' I mean creating material and work that I feel is a true representation of me. Whilst the majority of the poems in *An Obsessive Infatuation* had a foundation in real life, there were some that I felt less connected with.

This was not the case when I began to write my material for this book. I was writing for me, and only for me. All my thoughts, feelings, flights of fancy, highs and lows in my life, are in this book

A big difference between this book and *You. Are. Not. Alone.* and *An Obsessive Infatuation*, is that nothing is cut out. For me, that's a nice change, because when putting the previous books together, I had to cut out material that I felt was good, but did not have a place in the books for various reasons. And that was a pity. But not this time.

This book is me: the writer and the human being. I hope you enjoy this book.

Many thanks again,

W. R. Watkins

Contents

2015

2014

Ends Of The Earth
09/08/14

I want to follow you
to the ends of the Earth,
nothing coming between us,
just you and me,
both against the world,
and I promise you that I,
will protect you from all the hurt,
just as long as I can
follow you to the ends of the Earth.

I want to show everyone,
how much I love you,
that you're mine and my everything,
and if they have a problem with us,
we'll just shake them off because,
all that matters is what's between us,
and how it is simply more than pure love;
will follow you to the ends of the Earth.

Want to spend my days,
taking endless selfies with you in bed,
wake up early in the mornings,
with your head on my chest,
my arms wrapped around you,
till the day passes through,
not disturbing our little world;
will follow you to the ends of the Earth.
Going on the adventures we plan,
not questioning whether we can,
just going for it,

and taking in all the new experiences,
creating memories that we'll always share,
along with reminiscing during truth or dare,
Oh, how did I get so lucky?

I love you, and everything that you are.
I don't want to lose you to somebody else,
because you are the one for me,
you've given me more than I could imagine.
I want to show you, how much
you mean to me, how you've made me so happy.
I promise you that I won't ever give up on us.

All That Wealth
09/08/14

Diamonds, money,
fast cars, private jets,
country houses, vast estates,
chandeliers, ice cream vans,
Rolexes in abundance, holiday islands,
personal chefs, plus the trainer,
exclusive memberships, expensive tailors,
top of the range, big store brands.
With all that wealth, you could
buy whatever you want or can.

But there's one thing it can't buy,
and that is my heart.
Going to have to show me you're better,
if you really want there to be an 'us'.
I don't need your gifts,
your love is all that I want and need.
But if this is something you can't give,
then we aren't meant to be.

Impossible
09/08/14

Everything about you is impossible.
How can anyone be this beautiful?
Your smile could light up the world,
your eyes filled with a merriment and love.
So gorgeous no matter what you wear,
whether in your suit or your tracksuit,
and we'd still wind up in bed.
Your laughter captivates my soul,
could listen to you talk for hours,
about what I guess I'll never know,
because you're simply so distracting,
that I can't help but keep on staring,
taking in every detail of your face,
the way it crinkles when you smile,
to when it blushes when I pay you a compliment.
The way you look down in embarrassment,
is simply too cute and adorable,
that I can feel myself falling for you,
even though I know it's impossible,
to fall for someone so hard, for someone
so beautiful, but yet here I am,
falling deeper and deeper in love with you.

Back Into My Life
10/08/14

I can't believe it.
The moment I get over you,
you stroll back into my life,
as if nothing ever happened,
like we had meant nothing to each other.
I was once yours, and you were once mine.
And now what do I do?
I'm with someone else,
but got to try and forget you,
and it kills me every time,
I'm pulled away from you,
when all I want is to tell you everything,
so we can stop wasting time,
and just be together already.
Everything was so simple,
before you came back into my life,
and now everything reminds me
of all the wasted time we have.

Scar
10/08/14

I trace my fingertips over my scars,
that line my hands, wrists and stomach.
Visible reminders of when I felt weak,
when I thought I wouldn't make it,
to live to see another day.
Now I trace them over my heart,
and I feel the biggest scar,
that was made by you,
when you left, walking through the door,
tearing all of my love in half.
It's not a visible scar,
like the ones I made in my past.
But the pain still endures,
reminding me of how I wasn't enough,
how I wasn't enough for you,
to keep me in your life.
Oh this scar is the worst,
out of all my scars,
because I can physically feel,
the break you left in my heart.

Us
11/08/14

Can you please just talk to me?
Can't take you ignoring me any longer.
Instead of getting stronger, we're weaker,
steadily falling apart at the seams,
all of our future plans seem like hopeless dreams.
We seemed so strong, nothing could stop us,
how did we let the silence grow between us?
Slowly growing without resistance,
were we not worth fighting for?
Wasn't what we had strong enough?
Is there any future left for us?

Spectre
13/08/14

Spectre.
A ghost.
This is what you are to me.
Invisible.
Empty.
That is what we're becoming.
Silent words.
Broken promises.
What did I do deserve this?
Sometimes there.
Only in my mind.
You're just a spectre, lost in time.
Tears.
Pain.
You just keep bailing on me again and again.
I can't live life like this,
with you as a spectre,
so tired of playing this game.
You're either with me,
or you're leaving me.
Tell me now.

22/08/14

I put all that I was,
into my infatuation with you,
lost all my sense of reality,
for the chance to be with you.
And there you are,
crushing every dream I ever had over you.

Winter Nights
25/08/14

Autumn leaves return,
and the days grow cold,
I begin to reminisce about
those days of old.
When we used to play in the snow,
not having a care in the world,
creating snow angels,
nothing in the world could cause us hurt.
Laying in your arms,
on those cold winter nights,
gazing at the fire place,
thinking, "This is so right."
Watching the flickering flames,
wishing how we could freeze time,
let the world just slip us by,
so that this moment never ends.

Were The World Mine
29/08/14

Were the world mine,
I'd do almost anything,
to have you in my life.
Change the laws just for a chance,
to only have a little taste,
of our forbidden romance.
Run away with you,
away from prying eyes.
Oh, it would be perfect;
were the world mine.

Three Words
29/08/14

I want to say the words,
but they get caught in my throat.
They think it's so easy,
just to say those three words.
To open up your heart,
let them into your life, be brave enough.

Your Face
01/09/14

It's been so many years,
since I last saw your face.
And to be honest,
I thought I'd never have to, ever again.
But there you are, in all of your glory,
and I felt my old obsessive infatuation
begin to take over me.
Every detail about you is still the same,
and I remember how those little details,
used to bring heartache and pain.

Broken Goods
01/09/14

I'm nothing but broken goods,
shattered to pieces,
like splintered wood.
Don't get too close,
because I could hurt you,
give you a splinter,
from my unhealed wounds.
Why do you want me?
What is it about me,
that is still so appealing?

Why would you want to be,
with someone who is nothing more,
than broken goods?
You could have literally anybody,
yet you're still with someone,
whose soul is battered and bruised.

Did you really think,
that your love could save me?
(I'm beyond salvation)
Don't think that I didn't know,
it was all just pity.

03/09/14

There's no way you're going to escape me,
you're a permanent part of me,
so we're going to continue on in my mind,
maybe for all of eternity.

Tattoo
08/09/14

Can feel your fingers,
trailing an intricate pattern upon my skin,
making me want to burn it in,
like a tattoo,
make it permanent,
to remind me of that moment.

Fan Girl
08/09/14

Oh my God,
can't believe what you just did,
you talked to me,
and I lost all my sensibility.
If you could hear,
my inner fan girl,
squealing with absolute delight,
even though all you said to me
was just a simple, "Hi".
And instantaneously,
I was up on Cloud 9,
deliriously happy,
that you finally noticed me.

Puzzle Piece
08/09/14

I think you're my missing puzzle piece,
the part that completes my heart,
oh so perfectly.
Can see the picture we'd create,
so vividly in my mind's eye,
a perfect future together,
that will never have an end.

Still Own My Heart
14/09/14

It's been so long since we last met,
and I can still clearly see,
every single little detail of your face.
My heart still skips a beat,
when I think of you in my daydreams,
I guess you still own my heart,
even though you never knew it was yours.

Every day and every night,
I try to forget,
everything that I knew about you,
deleting our old texts,
burning all our pictures together,
yet you still own my heart.
I am stuck over what to do next.

What people don't understand,
is the angst that you feel,
something that is beyond description.
No matter how many times it's worded,
It's still not enough to effectively describe,
the hurt that seemingly lives on for forever.
And you still own my heart,
now I guess I'm just waiting for someone
to take over ownership from you,
give me back what I feel,
a love that is beyond real.

I Fucked Up
14/09/14

I fucked up.
I fucked up over you,
now I'm crying out,
screaming out for you to come back,
that what I did was wrong,
should have never done that.
I fucked us up,
please give me a second chance,
let me win your heart back,
prove to you I can be better,
never going to fuck this up again.
Please baby, come back to me,
don't abandon me.
Need you to survive.
Need you to breathe.
I fucked up,
forgive me for my sins,
take me back into your heart,
let's get back to what we used to be.

I fucked up.
I fucked up.

Negativity (School Yard Gossip)
14/09/14

It's amusing to me,
to think that you think,
that you can hurt me
like you used to,
but listen here darling,
got no time for your negativity.
Finally at a place in life,
where I am so happy,
that what you say,
does not even affect me.

And with all your little comments,
well say what you like,
to me they're just moments,
that have no place in my life.
Spreading nothing but negativity,
telling olden day stories,
I actually find it perplexing,
how they still have any validity.

And why are these stories still alive?
Have you been talking about me?
Am I still on your minds?
Why, thank you, I actually
don't know what to say,
all except for the fact,
I've never thought of you,
not once, for a single day.

Diary Of The Heart

So the fact you're still talking,
tells me so much about you,
obsessing over school yard gossip,
acting like it was the truth!
Well, you stick with your negativity,
I've got a life to love and live,
I still wish you well for the future,
and that you'll stop obsessing
over me eventually.

Second Thoughts
14/09/14

When you asked me to be your boyfriend,
I was overwhelmed by joy,
got a feeling that was strong,
stronger than I've ever felt before.
But now I'm so worried:
what if I'm not good enough for you?
That after a while, you will realize
that I am not as good as you thought,
wondering how to get out of this relationship,
your heart is no longer as eager as it once was,
losing interest in me, moving on to another one.
What if I'm not good enough for your folks,
that when you introduce me,
they think that it's just a joke?
I'm so scared that I won't be able to provide,
what it is that you want from life,
that I won't live up to your expectation,
leading to our destined separation.

Back In The Day
14/09/14

The spark that we once had,
may have flitted out and died,
but I firmly believe,
that our time will come again,
that we will fall back in love,
like how we did back in the day.
That passion we both had,
even though it has burnt away,
will come back stronger than ever,
because we believe in true love,
and if we're truly meant to be,
we'll find each other again one day,
fall back in love like back in the day.
We both know that we belong together,
that even if we find somebody else,
they won't compare to how we were,
it just wouldn't be the same,
we'd end up falling for each other,
like how we did, back in the day.

M. U. 2.
20/09/14

I got your Snapchat the other day,
not going to lie, but it brought
a smile to my face.
It only had a three worded caption,
that took my happiness to a new level,
and wrapping it up in a thick layer of rapture:

"Missing U 2night"

And with those three little words,
my feelings for you intensified,
maybe even giggled a little bit,
not felt like this for a long while.
It took me sometime, before I remembered,
that I had to reply to you,
so I simply sent one back saying:

"Missing U 2"

Military
21/09/14

Our love is like the military,
standing side by side united,
stronger than the strongest army.
No matter what they say,
no matter what they do,
we will always have each other,
supporting each other through and through.

Together we will always win,
even when the odds seem slim.
We're stronger together than apart,
they can't break out completed hearts.
Just like the military,
we both got our battle scars,
but in the end, we will be the victors,
stronger than ever before,
our love growing every dusk and dawn.

S.T.E.A.L.
02/10/14

She's taking everything and leaving
me with nothing, but a broken heart.
Wasn't my love enough for you?
What was it that I couldn't give you,
that she can seemingly give so easily?
Trying to ascertain where we went wrong,
why didn't I see what she had been
doing for so long, going behind my back,
whispering in your ear,
stealing you away from my heart.

The Boy I Fell In Love With
03/10/14

I don't know who you are,
not the same boy I once loved,
who came in, swept me off my feet,
overcame everything I put in your way,
and eventually stole my heart.

Where did that boy go?
Is he still in there somewhere?
How can I help you to remember,
of how we used to be together?
Of those dates we went on,
whispering to each other,
of how we never wanted those nights to end?
Saying how happy we'd become,
now that we were more than friends?

But now, that joy has left your eyes,
and a cold cruelty has taken you over,
leaving me paralysed with fear,
of what you could do to me,
shaking at the memory of what you did,
when I was late back just one evening.

You're not the boy I fell in love with,
somehow, somewhere along the lines,
that boy who could make me laugh at anything,
left this world and changed his life,
determined to make mine a misery.
Oh, how I wish I could fix you,
change you back to how you were,
back to the boy I fell in love with,
before this horrible change occurred.

I Know You
17/08/14

I know you,
every single part of you,
living with you vicariously,
and all you've been through.

I know you,
maybe more than you do,
listening to you so closely,
pretty sure you never had a clue.

I know you.

13/10/14

I guess I had this preconception,
of what it would be like with you.
Visions of only the beautiful things,
filling every crevasse of my imagination,
ignoring that gut feeling,
that there could be something wrong with you.
I turned away from the possibility,
that you wouldn't be,
how I had imagined you to be,
now I guess I was proven to be right,
that there was another side to you,
something I was blind to from the start.

Oh why did I give you my heart?
Why didn't I listen to my head?
No amount of wishing you to change,
will amount to anything that I could
grasp onto, to keep this dream alive.
The denial that we are finished,
is blocking me from being brave,
stopping me from moving away from you.

You're Mine
13/10/14

It feels so different this time,
the feelings mutually returned,
finally hearing somebody whispering
those two words I longed to hear.

"You're mine."

Loved Like That
14/10/14

Sitting in the car,
listening to Little Things,
and I can't help but wonder,
why can't I be loved like that?
Where all my flaws are positive,
in my partner's eyes,
that they make me stronger,
just by saying that they love me,
no matter how society views me.
Where they brush away a fallen tear,
as I sit there listening to their words,
feeling comforted and so much love,
that gradually I begin to believe,
that all those beautiful words,
are truly meant only for me.

23/10/14 (I)

I'm losing you for forever.
I can feel my heart shattering;
this is more than I can bear.
It's at times like this,
I wish that I never had
any feelings for you.
I guess my fear of everlasting solitude,
is all coming true,
I'm losing you, to someone
who is so much better than me.
It's almost funny actually,
when I think of all those dreams,
of you and me, that will
never come to be.
I'm losing you, and I can feel my heart
physically breaking.

23/10/14 (II)

Can't you see my heart bleeding out,
an outpouring of love,
that is only meant for you to see,
of how I feel towards you.
Trying so desperately,
to de-visualise your face from my mind,
to give me a fighting chance to break free,
from this enchanting grip,
you have over me.

23/10/14 (III)

Walking across a floor,
seemingly made of stars,
my mind begins to wander,
and I wonder where you are.

Am I at the forefront of your mind,
like you are on mine nearly constantly?
Or am I just a faded picture,
that has merged with other memories?
Sometimes in the mornings,
I murmur out your name,
secretly hoping that miles away,
you'll somehow hear me.

Blank Canvas
01/11/14

Treat me as your blank canvas,
tell me what has been troubling you,
for so long, so much.
I know when something is wrong,
it's so plain for me to see,
it pains me to see you unhappy,
and know that I can do nothing.

Treat me like your blank canvas,
paint all your troubles on me,
get them out of your system,
and I will always listen to you,
no matter the time of the day.

Treat me as your blank canvas,
talk to me about everything,
will never judge you,
(how could I?)
help you through the best way,
I think I can.

One. Two. More.
01/11/14

One. Two. More.
The tears begin to fall.
Three. Four. Five.
They keep welling up inside.
A waterfall down my face,
each tear leaving a trace,
a path of my sadness,
that is now out of control.

One. Two. More.
I sit here waiting for your call.
Three. Four. Five.
The hours pass mockingly slowly,
each minute feeling like eternity,
just waiting for you to phone,
and tell me I'm the one you love more.

Love Notes
01/11/14

It doesn't seem so long ago,
that I was yours, you were mine,
having a summer love,
that we wished would never end.
Writing those love notes,
passing them back and forth,
always risking getting caught,
but they made us so happy,
that we never really cared.
Sneaking in little kisses,
in those brief moments,
that only in our minds,
lasted for a lifetime,
breaking apart reluctantly,
to continue with our masquerade.

But eventually we parted ways,
promising that we would stay in touch.
And at first we did,
texting each other late into the night,
never getting enough from one and another,
to say the words "Goodnight."
But ever so gradually,
we slowly texted even less.
Somehow we were always busy,
having no time for each other,
forgetting what we once meant
ever so dearly to each other.

But those love notes lingered on,
collecting dust,
in my secret box of things,
sometimes re-reading them,
on those rainy days,
and smile as I reminisce,

and realize how much I miss you.
 I miss you so much.
The love notes keep me going,
until I can finally touch you again,
feel you against my skin,
write all new love notes,
pass them again secretly,
reaffirming what we once felt for each other.

Sh!t Talkers
01/11/14

People talk shit all the time,
something about them
wants to degrade other people's lives.
Either way, what they say,
won't change how I see you in my own eyes.
It's going to take more,
than basic shit talking,
for my opinion to change.
You have your faults,
and there is no denying it,
but the thing is,
so do I, and so does
everybody else around us.
The faults with us,
are a part of who we are,
and we can't pick or choose
the qualities that we like.
Because ultimately,
we'll end up disappointed,
that the person before us,
is not how we imagined.
But I can see you, every single fault,
and in all honesty,
you're still the same
perfection that I fell in love with,
all of those years ago.
The shit talkers haven't said,
anything I don't know already,
so there is nothing that they can say,
to change the way I feel about you.

The way I've felt for you day after day.

Surrender
01/11/14

I surrender.

I wave my white flag.
I can't keep up the fight.
I'm clearly disadvantaged,
by an opponent so much better.
Guess I've always known in my heart,
that we were finished long ago,
but I clung to that distant hope,
that somehow we could reignite,
that spark that was once there.
But now, I understand,
I should now be the gracious man,
and let you live your life.

I surrender.

Smoke & Mirrors
23/11/14

No more magic tricks,
just a plain honesty.
Removing the mask,
so you can see me,
for whom I really am.
No smoke & mirrors,
just me in all that I am.
I only put on the play,
just to make you feel safe,
but I can see that was a mistake.
I should have been honest,
right from our beginning.
Could we start over,
and I promise no tricks,
re-build our relationship
on just trust and honesty?

Proclamation of Love
23/11/14

I need you,
I need you with me.
I can't survive,
if you leave me,
I know I'll die.

You make me strong,
like I'm doing something right,
finally got something good,
that I've got in my life.
If you leave me,
everything that I am,
will surely end.

I can't lose you,
I promise to make it better,
treat you with the love
that you should always get.
You're my soul, my love,
everything that I love to please.

Beautiful Picture
26/11/14

Where did we go wrong?
I don't know where all this
hostility is coming from.
Was I foolish enough,
not to see this coming for us?
How the rift in our bed,
has slowly been growing over time?
And yet now we are here,
throwing out the words,
that we don't really mean,
slowly falling more and more apart,
unravelling at the seams,
until our beautiful picture,
that was once so perfect,
is shredded and scattered,
much like our now broken dreams.

28/11/14

I go so caught up in the lies,
that I never realised that I,
was slowly hurting you.
With each day that passes,
denying continually how I feel.
In my head, I thought that I
was protecting you in some way.
That if I said that I felt nothing,
I would eventually believe those words,
but instead the opposite occurred,
and steadily fell more in love with you.
But now, the damage has been done,
said those words enough, that
you've moved on with your life,
and I'm now stuck here, feeling bitter regret,
wishing that I could take back,
each and every denial that I said,
just for the chance to have you back.

Christmas Love
Started: 29/11/14; Finished: 30/11/14

The Christmas lights,
bring a festive joy,
to the packed street.
Shoppers moving through
the flurries of snow,
without a glance, at me and you.
We hold tight to each other,
and just like the snow,
we fall deeper and deeper,
and deeper in love,
our hands intertwined,
and I can't think of a reason to be,
anywhere else but here with you.

30/11/14 (I)

There is a bitter touch,
in this winter night air,
sending chills to the bone,
that is almost too much to bear.
The carols float softly,
all through the air,
creating a Christmas spirit,
that releases all your
past worries and cares.
Glad tidings passed around,
lovers under the mistletoe,
their lips making the only sound,
telling you of their love,
that has stood against the
tests of time this year.

30/11/14 (II)

Oh, look at the snow,
falling so gently outside.
The Christmas tree,
filled with all its lights,
creating quite a sight.
And a sense of tranquillity,
descends upon you,
all tensions alleviated,
preparing you to start anew,
for all the surprises the
New Year is to bring.

Love Interest
30/11/14

Love can be such a fickle thing.
One minute you're in so deep,
that you can't see yourself,
being with anybody else in your life.

But the next day it's verging on
ever so nearly being over,
that you feel so alive, that
you know this is the end.

Some can play the love game,
moving from one to another,
without so much of a second thought.
But others wait in solitude,
waiting for the right person,
to come into their life,
that they can give their all to.

Whilst others stay, because
they feel there is no escape;
that there is nothing better for them,
and that is where they are wrong.
Because the one who wishes
that they could love them dearly,
has to look on from a distance,
with that dream where one day,
their love interest notices them,
and for all that they are.

Finally giving you the chance,
to give them all your heart,
allowing that secret romance
a start and the chance to flourish,
and take flight, out of the
shadows, bringing your love
into all that is good and right.

In Too Deep
30/11/14

I guess that somewhere in my heart,
I've come to terms with reality,
that what I wish we could have,
will never in fact, ever will be.
That our hands will never touch,
intertwining in the most intimate way.
That the loving words, that I
so desperately want you to say,
never will be said to me.
I will have to give up on everything,
that I wish and dream we could be.
Can't simply do what I did last time,
can't bring myself to cut you from my life.
We're in too deep, connections are
now so intricate, that to sever them,
will almost certainly kill me.

30/11/14 (III)

Both of us are dancing around the truth,
not wanting to admit our feelings,
scared that the other will not feel the same,
and that we can't go through,
that feeling of rejection all over again.

Precious time slips us by,
time we could have had together,
instead we conceal continually,
that we feel something for each other.

And that time turns into years,
with us still too afraid,
still harbouring our feelings at night,
thinking that they will never love us,
and that we have got nothing,
that they would ever want.

But then comes that fateful day,
when we both find the courage,
to say how we feel finally,
and tears of relief flow,
when we hear those precious words,
saying that they feel the same.

Heart On My Sleeve
03/12/14

I'm wearing my heart on my sleeve,
just to prove how much you mean to me.
And if that is not enough to convince you,
tell me whatever it is that I have to do,
so that you believe me when I say "I love you."
Shower you with everything that I have got,
but somehow that doesn't seem to be enough.
I whisper all those tender things to you at night,
and yet you pull away, your insecurities
nullifying everything that I try.
I'm getting desperate, don't know what to do,
got my heart on my sleeve here,
give me at least a sign, give me a clue.

Reflective Moment
07/12/14

There are still those days,
where I wish I could go back,
do things differently.
Make the changes to my life
that could be beneficial,
but in the long run they
could make my life more difficult.
But then I stop to really think,
about my life currently,
about the people in it and
my whole perspective changes.
Yes, my life would be different,
but not in the way I think it would.
I would not have the people I have
let get so close to my heart,
stuck to wonder what I would have
done without them from the start.
Even if I made one change,
I do believe there is a chance,
that I wouldn't have survived.
Lack the strength so many others have,
to live their lives on.

The Battlefields
07/12/14

We were destined for each other,
And be friends no matter what.
Reunited once more on the battlefields
Holding each other with everything we got.
Our determination keeping us strong
Resisting those who doubt our purpose,
Setting out to be together against the odds,
Eventually together again on the battlefields.

A Little While
07/12/14

Why do you have to leave tonight?
Stay with me for a little while longer.
Let us have this moment,
for as long as we can have it,
stay with me for a little while longer.
There is no rush for us,
time is something we have an abundance of.
You can stay with me,
for as long as you want to.

Secrets In The Bedroom
07/12/14

There is something between us,
there are secrets in the bedroom,
that we aren't saying to each other,
tell me what has been troubling you.

I can see it in your eyes,
can read between the lines,
that all that you're saying to me,
is nothing more than lies.

I wait patiently for you to tell me,
to reveal the truth eventually,
but every day that passes for me,
another crack in my heart appears.

Each time you walk out of the door,
another tear escapes from me,
wondering if you'll return,
if you'll come back to me.

Never once have I doubted you,
but lately all my doubts have grown,
the secrets in the bedroom,
are expanding by the hour,
don't know if I can live,
knowing of the growing void
that is destroying us.

Secrets in the bedroom.

Scent
07/12/14

Every room I walk into,
your scent is everywhere.
As I pack your clothes away,
it becomes beyond overwhelming.
Each shirt that I fold away,
breaks me down in so many ways,
as your scent transports me
to all those old tucked away memories.
Every moment we had together,
both the good and the bad,
your scent transports me back
to when we had everything.

But now you're gone.
And your scent is all I have left.
No more memories to be made,
now that you've been lain to rest.
I pray that your scent never fades,
I'm not ready to let you go yet.

All those autumn walks,
through the cold winter air,
laying down next to you,
I can (almost) feel you still there.
All your jumpers, I press to my face,
inhaling all that you were,
I'm just turning into a mess.
Your scent comforts me,
and I can (almost) feel your arms,
bringing me the safety that you
used to bring to me.

The bed is so much colder,
no longer have your warmth.
The days melt into the nights,
soldering into one blur,
and yet it only feels like yesterday,
the day that I felt the most hurt,
the day that I lost you.

I sleep with your clothes,
wrapping myself up with your scent,
but it will never be the same,
will never wake up in the mornings,
to be greeted by your face.
People try to get me out,
but nothing seems worth living for.
You were my rock,
the stability I needed, to be
able to keep going on.

Your scent lingers over everything,
every surface that I touch,
sometimes I feel like I'm dreaming,
that all that has happened,
has no place in my reality,
that you're still here with me,
and that your scent is not the
only thing, keeping you alive for me.

Cheater
08/12/14

I don't know how you can
live with yourself,
knowing you've been cheating on me.
You think I don't know?
Well I found his clothes hidden
all around our home,
how long has this been going on for?
I thought that maybe, it was
only that one time, and I let
it slip by, thinking nothing more of it.
But now you can barely be
in the same room as me,
spending more time with him,
and the pieces fall together instantly.
I know that I'm hurting,
but can't bring myself to leave you,
doing anything to prove to you
that I love you more than he ever could.
Where did I go wrong?
What did I do to drive you to him?
When did you get tired of me,
to become a low life cheater?

The Path
08/12/14

The path towards acceptance,
can be a long one indeed.
Some people find it easily,
whilst others take their time.
The fear of what others say,
hinder our personal journey,
stopping us from progressing,
down the path of accepting,
that part of us that sets us apart,
from the rest of society.
And even though by now,
it shouldn't have to be this way,
there is still a taboo attached,
to when someone comes out as gay.
But, no matter what happens,
we love and accept you.
(And I shouldn't have to write that)
Your path of acceptance,
will lead you to better places,
to a life where you're no longer afraid,
no matter if you're straight, bi or gay.

Concrete Walls
12/12/14

You're trying to break down
my concrete walls,
bringing all my anxiety to
a whole new level.
Making me feel my inferiority,
putting on the pressure
I've been desperately avoiding.

I can feel the judging stares,
bearing down on me,
but my concrete walls are
barely crumbling,
stopping the words that
are wanting to be formed,
making me think you're
disappointed in me even more.

The screams in my head,
are telling me to get out,
this is too much to bear.
Why can't you see that
I can't speak about me?
That my concrete walls
are preventing me from
opening up all the way,
saying the words that I really
wish that I could say.

And it hurts me so much,
that I almost begin to cry.
The tears are there, and
I'm willing them to dry so that
you don't see, that vulnerable
side of me, which is threatening
to break out, making me
scream and shout:
"Why are you doing this to me?!"

Please stop breaking into my inner mind,
I know this may hurt you,
but it is going to take time,
before I feel comfortable enough,
to reveal the thoughts in my mind.

What you don't know is that
it is so hard for me to say,
o I write out the words
here instead, in the hope
that one day you'll realise,
that I'm not normal,
I'm not like the other guys,
because I let my concrete walls,
throw up those barriers,
that have been in place for years,
to stop people using my fears,
making a mockery of me,
and I know it's so silly
to be thinking like this,
but that is just how it is.

And I won't get any better,
if you keep up this relentless
attack on my exterior,
hoping that I will open up to you,
let my concrete walls down,
only just because it's you.
It's not that easy,
I can assure you.

Be Patient With Me
12/12/14

I feel attacked on all sides,
feel pressurised to be someone,
someone I have never been,
for most of my life.

How can you expect me,
to simply open up and reveal,
a vulnerability that is my feelings,
that I have held inside for so long?

I simply can't do it,
as easily as you think,
can't verbalise the emotions,
running through my mind.

If I could do it,
don't you think I'd have done it?
Long before we talked,
how can I help you understand this?

You say that I take for granted,
all that we have,
sorry to disappoint you (again),
but I'm not like that.

I'm fully aware of all I have,
and to hear you think I don't,
hurts me so much,
you can barely imagine.

Diary Of The Heart

What I realised today,
is how much you don't know me,
misunderstand me,
disappointed in me.
You think this hurts you?
Think how this interrogation
is hurting me.
You're breaking me.

Once again on my own,
defending myself,
you're no better than the others,
claiming you want to help me.

You say we should be open,
that we need to communicate more often,
it just feels the opposite,
like that you're ganging up on me.

Forcing me into a position,
that makes me feel uncomfortable,
with no regard as to whether or not,
I find what you're asking of me is difficult.

And even then I can't say that,
because I know you'll disregard it,
pressing on me further,
to just get over it.
And you wonder why I rarely open up,
it doesn't feel safe for me to do so,
not yet in a place where I feel,
ready enough to let it go.

But in the end, I know you'll disregard
all the words written here,
try to validate your reasons,
but I just don't want to hear.

Chains
12/12/14

You got me wrapped in chains,
but I'm never going away,
you can lock me up,
throw away the key.
I never intend to break away
from these restraints.
I'm yours; nobody else's,
I'm not going to leave these chains.

Dominated My Life
14/12/14

I fell for you too hard,
fell for you too fast,
and now I'm paying the price,
for giving my heart away,
to a guy I thought that I
wouldn't have had to think twice about.
Was it my gullibility,
that made it so easy?
Letting you into my broken heart
(under the guise of mending it)
so you could break me,
seemingly so easily apart.
Depended on what I knew about you,
from all those years ago,
not once stopping to think,
that you could be different,
that you were the same boy,
who dominated my life,
for such a long, long time.

What Did I Say?
14/12/14

What did I say for you to turn away?
What did I say for you to hate me?
What did I say to deserve a slammed door?
What did I say for you to stop loving me anymore?
What did I say for you to scream?
What did I say for you to act so mean?
What did I say for you to ignore me?
What did I say to deserve these reprimands?
What did I say for this to become so difficult?

What did I say?

Lost Chance
15/12/14

A lost chance,
I guess that's what you are to me.
A missed opportunity,
to give our romance a chance.
And now you're with someone else.
I'm here, looking on from a distance,
my heart pounding,
screaming out only your name.
You're my lost chance,
so now I'm left alone with only the pain.
Do you think one day,
we will ever be together?
Make up for the lost time,
that we could have had with each other?
Or are we completely over,
with no chance of ever being one heart,
holding each other like we wish to do?

Or are you just my lost chance?

17/12/14 (I)

People turn to me for comfort,
and I let them cry on my shoulder,
because I hate seeing my friends hurt.
But every once in a while,
there are those days when I need
a shoulder to cry on,
but I feel like I'm interrupting their lives.
(How many times have I
privately written that line?)
They're just trivial problems,
that usually just fade away,
except there are those that
linger on in my head,
filling it with the words that
are full of self-hate.
And it's those words that are
so hard for me to erase,
going round and around in a loop,
the self-hate seeping through
every cell in me, making me believe,
that hate that I can't escape.

17/12/14 (II)

Sometimes in our lives,
we find ourselves,
in a permanent rewind.
Where nothing moves forward,
making the same mistakes,
our visions for the future disillusioned.

Voices
20/12/14

Voices.
Whispering;
Circling;
Attacking;
Unrelenting;
Hating;
Harming;
Destroying;
Confusing;
Listening;
Believing;
Ending;
Killed.

Fast Lane
22/12/14

Slow down,
ease up on the gas,
you're passing through life,
a little too fast.
Take in what's around you,
really feel each experience,
and truly appreciate,
the meaning of this existence.
Take yourself out of the fast lane,
slow things down a little bit,
and enjoy all that you have
so far accomplished,
and know that each day,
doesn't have to be the same.

Time
22/12/14

It's the only thing that does not wait,
does not care if you're early or late.
Nothing can defeat this inevitable power,
commands all that we do every hour.
It can take away, it cannot bring back,
a cold cruelty which lacks,
any sort of empathy for its victims,
who plead for a little compassion,
to spend a while longer with a loved one.
But no, time has no heart.
It is nothing but an unrelenting force,
that constantly reminds us,
how fickle and small we truly are,
compared to the vastness of the universe.

The Impossible Gift (Last Christmas)
26/12/14

I can remember so clearly,
our last Christmas.
Play those memories over again,
as I look through the pictures.
How little did we know,
what the year to come,
was going to bring us?
How that was going to be,
our last Christmas

I can remember sitting to the side,
watching you unwrap your presents.
I've never seen such a huge smile,
thanking people so many times,
but beyond all that,
I was blessed to call you mine.

I can still hear your laughter,
echoing all around me,
and a little bit more dies inside me,
when I realise that I,
will never hear it ever again.
All my future Christmases,
will never be the same.

I can remember the walk on Boxing Day,
when you held my hand all the way,
still sneaking in those glances at me,
when you thought that I wouldn't see,
how you still turned your head,

smiling and looking so cute blushing.

I remember, how you gave me
the very last gift to give,
saying you had a question for me.
And as you got down on one knee,
I could not help but start crying,
and as those four words,
tumbled from your sweet lips,
I could barely speak,
as I nodded, making you the
happiest person I have ever seen.

So, as I stare down,
at that beautiful stone,
still set upon my finger,
I begin to regret and wonder,
of all the things we could have been.
For me, there is no one else,
that will ever compare to you.
I don't know how you expect me,
to move on from you,
because I don't think I will ever
be ready to love someone again,
especially to the point where losing them,
can cause me so much pain.

That was our last Christmas together,
and now you're gone,
there won't be any more for us.
So I spend this Christmas Day,
wishing, just wishing for the impossible gift,
that is for you to be returned to me.

Small Building Block
28/12/14

This poem is for...

...anyone who has ever been
told that they're not good enough.
...anyone who was made to feel
small, unimportant, worthless.
...anyone who was made to feel
inferior to those around them.
...anyone who has felt lost,
alone and afraid.
...anyone who has felt like they won't
want to continue with this life.

You are not any of those things.
You are worth more than you think.
Someday, you will look back,
feel at peace with what has been,
and realize that what you went through,
was a small building block of your life,
a life that has grown to be beautiful.

Don't let the bullies in,
don't let the tormentors win.
I know life seems so hopeless,
that the pain you feel,
makes you feel degraded even less
than what the bullies are saying.

But they are wrong,
and so are you.
Take my word for it,
when I say you're going to
pull through, and that
your pain will ebb away,
making room for the happiness
you'll feel every day.

And even though,
I have never met you,
or that I don't know you're name.
I've felt and shared your pain,
and trust me when I say that
it will only be temporary.
Things will get better,
promise me you'll hold on to
that faith, that you'll makes sure,
that you fight to live another day.

2015

Search For Love
01/01/15

Ok, that's enough.
Time to get off my arse,
and search for love.
I'm not going to let it be,
year after year,
just being only me.
I want to find somebody,
whom I can share my life with,.
Searching for that someone,
whom I can share my heart with.
I'm no longer content,
to just being on my own,
I want to be with someone at last,
proving I'm not destined to be alone.
He's out there,
I can feel it in my soul.
It's time I searched for love,
let's give it a go!

Wait For You (Forever)
03/01/15

I can wait for you for forever,
doesn't matter how long it takes,
I'll wait until you're ready.
Just know that you've got my love,
that you already have my heart.
I've loved you for so long already,
a few more months don't matter to me.

I can wait for you for forever,
because I know it would be worth it;
that what we could potentially be,
would be worth the wait for you.
I've never stopped loving you,
even when I thought there was no hope,
no matter what I tried to do,
nothing could rid you from my mind.

And now that there is a possibility,
that we could have our shot,
saying that you need some time,
that's fine by me.
Just let me know when you're ready,
but know that I'll wait for you for forever.
You'll always have my love.

Late Night Ramblings
04/01/15

I hate myself.

I mean, what is there to like?
I look in the mirror,
and all I see staring back at me,
is nothing more than an ugly sight.
My skin is blotchy,
my teeth all crooked and nasty,
my hair does what it likes,
no matter how hard I try to change it.
I feel so big, that I can understand,
why no one would want to be with
this lump of broken mess.
So messed up in my head,
talking to nobody or anybody,
living in the visions that I wish
can be my true reality.

I'm done.

Nobody will ever want me.
And why would they?
Why would they want to be with,
a loser like me?
Why would somebody put themselves
through the torture of being my boyfriend?
I wouldn't.
I wouldn't even give me a second glance.
I plaster a smile on my face,
re-apply my worn out mask.
It's so used I bet people can see right
through it, and see the broken,
dejected spirit that inhabits this shell.

A shell.

I guess that's what I really am.
A vehicle of nothingness,

that tries to trick itself into believing,
that its life has some purpose.
Why couldn't I be normal?
Why couldn't I simply just be normal?
Maybe then I wouldn't be alone.
Maybe instead of 2 decades worth of
nothing but a loneliness,
maybe I would have somebody I could be with.
Somebody who might say "I love you",
giving me back what I feel for them.
But instead, I'm force to look
at those I like from so far,
that I'd bet that they don't even know,
that I exist.

Do you know, what's it like,
to see people your own age,
already settling down,
marrying or getting engaged?
And here I am.
With nothing to live for.
What's the point in having all of this,
if I've got nobody special,
whom I can share it all with?
What's the point?
What's the point?

Don't say that it will happen for me.
There is no use in lying to me,
or covering up the truth of the matter.
I finally am realising,
where it is in society,
that my place is.
And that is, to be the outsider,
forever cursed to be looking in.
get it now, so now I've got to
just live with it.

I'm just so tired of wanting so much,
to get so very little in return,
that I don't even know what is worse anymore.

The hurt of continual disappointment?
Or the hurt of a continually shattered heart.

There is only a small part of me left,
that wants to believe that I am
meant to be loved by someone.
A dying hope, gasping for breath,
as reality slowly suffocates it to death.
My dreams of love, continue to try
and bring it back to a full fire and life.
But with each passing day,
it slowly dies a little bit more,
along with more of my heart,
which has been shattered too many times.

Enough!

Enough with these rambling thoughts.
Get yourself together.
Don't forget all that you've
managed to accomplish.
Remember how your life was so
much more miserable,
that all you could dream about,
was one day having friends?
Well didn't that dream come true,
or was it all just pretend?
If that one dream could come true,
then why not for your newest wish?

It may take it's time with you,
but you need to truly believe that
eventually, one day, it will.

And you know what?
I think it will be worth the wait.
That it will be everything you've
ever wished for, I mean it.
Don't give up on your hope,
let it propel you forward.

And who knows,
eventually, you may end up
finding the perfect somebody,
before this year's end.

Don't you dare give up.

Don't lose your faith in life.

It's given you so much already,
just let it take it's time.

Questions & Doubts
07/01/15

Another early morning,
where I find myself thinking,
about all the worries and doubts,
that are flying through my mind.
Have I made the right decision?
Is it too late, is there no more time?
I find myself doubting,
every career decision I've made.
Have I gone down the right path?
Will this eventually work out?
Or is this all just a terrible mistake.

I hope that the answers,
to all my questions and doubts,
soon present themselves to me.
Because I'm beginning to fear,
that I'll quickly fade into irrelevancy,
that everything I've worked to achieve,
would have all been for nothing.

Unfinished Words
10/01/15

There are days when I feel,
I never got the chance,
to say a proper goodbye.
That never again,
will I get the chance,
to speak to you in this life.
It all happened,
so very suddenly,
that I still can't comprehend it.
I guess, if I had the chance,
for one last talk with you,
I'd make the most of it,
telling you everything,
saying those unfinished words,
that I desperately wish,
I could say to you now.

Second Guesses
11/01/15

Why do I feel so worthless,
when you second guess me?
Why do you make me feel,
as if I can't do anything?
Working hard for results,
but for it seems it's not enough.
That even the good news I have,
you make it seem so bad.
You seem to think I've done nothing,
that the slow progress I've made,
seems so insignificant.

I'm sorry I've lived under,
all of your expectations.
That I am a seeming failure,
a source of aggravation,
that is not going away.
All the plans I've made,
I can see slipping from me,
disappearing down the drain,
resigning myself to the fact,
that everything I want in life,
will never be good enough for you.

All my self-confidence,
shattered to smithereens.
Do you know that feeling,
where you think you're doing ok,
and somebody comes along,
and ruins everything.

Isn't it strange as well,
that you get more support,
from complete and total strangers,
and yet you get nothing more,
than just a "Good" or "Well done",
from within your own home?

It makes me feel so small,
like I did all those months ago,
and the fact that I'm feeling this way,
because of my own family,
makes it so much more difficult,
for me to deal with.
If it had been because of anybody else,
I would be able to rationalise it,
making it so much easier to deal with.

But all of these second guesses,
are driving me insane,
can slowly steadily feel,
that well of self-doubt,
opening up all over again.

That I'm not good for anything.
That I'm not worth a thing.

13/01/15

Sometimes you won't get the things you want.
Sometimes you have to make concessions.
But sometimes, you have to ignore the doubts,
and push on forward.

(Insert Name)
14/01/15

(Insert name),
I wish that I could tell you,
everything I've ever wanted to say.
How strongly I feel for you,
and yet, I can't write your name.
If I had the option,
I would let it all out,
say it in the open,
but every force in my body,
pulls those words away from my mouth,
and passes them down to my pen.

(Insert name),
this ache I consistently feel,
overwhelms me day and night.
Overrides my heart and mind,
and I'm pulled into those memories,
of the time I first laid eyes on you.
My heart still skips,
even over those replayed memories,
and I smile for a bit,
forgetting that that is all they'll be.

(Insert name),
last night I dreamt about you,
about how we danced the night away.
You held me so close,
whispering in my ear,
letting go of all the words,
I still dream to one day hear.

It was just us, alone in the room,
dancing to the music,
that we both loved so much.

(Insert name),
I try to move on from you.
But I fail every single day.
You'd think it would be easy,
to let go of what you never had,
but the heart wants what it wants,
and it never lets go easily.
It doesn't want to hurt again,
so it refuses to accept the truth,
that the daydreams you have,
are only there to protect you.

(Insert name),
please say the words,
that I never want to hear.
Tell me nothing will happen,
and walk away, ignoring my tears.
The hurt should be enough for my heart,
to know that this is all real,
and maybe, it will finally let you go.

(Insert name),
help me. Please.

Prisoner
16/01/15

I feel like a prisoner,
an inmate with no chance in Hell,
of every being able to escape.
My cell walls are decorated
by myself in the hopes to mask,
how very trapped I've now become.
I feel so empty,
a hopelessness that is on the rise,
that I can feel who I am,
being stripped away time after time.
The phone rings,
reminding me that I can't be on my own,
when that's the very thing I want,
some time for me just being alone.
To reclaim who I am,
both in body and mind,
but I'm just a prisoner,
just doing my time.

Coming Out
16/01/15

How can I describe to you,
how I feel right now?
Which words do I choose,
so I get the right response out?
You see, I've written it so many times,
one day, I'll run out of rhymes,
trying to convey what I really feel,
what I'm tired of trying to conceal.

There is a part of me,
that has been securely locked away,
that I so desperately want to come out,
let the people close to me,
know whom I'd like to ask out.
That maybe then I can live my life,
out in the open air,
no longer worrying about being revealed,
that is all I can dream about.

My friends already know,
and they still want to know me,
I'm forever grateful to them,
but I know that eventually,
I'll have to tell other people about
my little secret.
And I hope that they don't hate me for it.

You see, I tried to do it with Alone,
but second thoughts got the better of me.
And now here I am, now wondering,

will I ever have the strength to say
those three words, ever again?

I know that it's pointless to think,
About what may never happen.
Maybe they'll figure it out,
Give me the satisfaction of not saying
Anything directly to them,
You never know what may happen.

If you've figured it out,
I hope that you understand,
I'm not doing this to hurt you,
but because this is who I am.
If you haven't yet,
I suggest that you read on,
because clearly you aren't
supposed to know yet,
but one day the realisation will dawn.
Please, don't hate me.

You Time
20/01/15

Sometimes, you just need to stop,
breathe, relax, gather yourself,
and give yourself some love.

20/01/15

If I could,
you'd be the one,
that I'd choose to be with.

Forbidden Fruit
20/01/15

I want to move on,
but my heart tugs me back,
you're the forbidden fruit,
I wish I could have.

No More Tears
21/01/15

That's it.
No more tears for you.
Enough have fallen,
stained my face red,
and nothing will come of them,
so needlessly wasted,
on someone clearly not worth my time,
on someone not worth waiting for,
for the rest of my life.
I thought I loved you once,
so much that it physically hurt,
even more than when you left me.

So you have had your tears,
time to move on from you.

No more tears.

3-way
21/01/15

When our hearts are tied in a three-way,
one will always be burned in some way.
Left on the side, whilst the other two,
happily have what the third wants to have,
in some way or another.
A small tear appearing in its muscle wall,
why does life have to be so cruel,
to let one heart out of three be damaged,
and left wanting (and deserving) so much more?

The second heart out of the three,
remains ignorant to the discarded heart,
never knowing of its secret needs and wants,
thinking that everything is ok, when in reality,
the discarded heart's strings are breaking,
no longer playing the happy sound they played,
when they sang the tune of being in love.

The final heart in the three-way tug,
remains smug over the victory,
having obtained the prize it thinks it deserves,
knowing that this is killing the first heart.
Therefore it does everything it can,
to make sure that the first heart is in pain,
by mistreating whom it desires,
driving the knife deeper into the wound,
whilst also masquerading as the loving partner,
hoping that the second heart remains none-the-wiser.

Finally
22/01/15

"I love you."

There they are, the words that I wanted to hear
for so long from you, I was beginning to fear,
that it would never eventually happen,
that everything we've been through,
had been all for nothing.

"I love you too."

And those words I've dreamed of saying,
slip from my lips so naturally,
I did not even have to think twice,
let the moment sweep me up and away,
still think this is a scene from my mind.

We pull each other close,
and the desperation begins to show,
kissing each other the way we've always wanted.
Feeling each other's excitement grow,
getting harder and harder for the both of us,
never wanting to let the other go.

Our lips briefly part,
and we gaze into each other's eyes,
getting lost in their iridescence,
feeling so euphoric about finally revealing,
all those buried emotions to each other,
making us feel like we're transcendent
about everybody else.

You take me by the hand,
and lead me away,
up to your room, asking me to stay.
And that night,
we gave ourselves to each other,
so many times over till morning light,
where I found myself,
wrapped in your arms,
my head against your chest,
finally at that stage in my life,
where I can be your boyfriend,
and not just your ordinary friend.

My Resolution
23/01/15

Sometimes I fuck up,
sometimes I make mistakes,
but I do what I think it takes,
to get to my final goals,
taking no prisoners as I go,
internally knowing that this path,
that I'm forging so carefully,
is one I need to travel along alone.

Burning some bridges,
fortifying others,
keeping that I can about,
truly close to my heart,
because they're all I've got,
they made me who I am.
If I ever stray to the side,
I know they will guide me
back to the right side of life,
giving me the strength to go on.

People doubt my intentions,
that the path I've taken,
is not the conventional one to take,
but I believe with every fibre,
of every part of my being,
that this is right for me,
no doubts in my mind,
of where I am going,
and I know it is going to be tough,
but in my spirit I know,
that this is the direction I need to go.

Maybe One Day... (Spread Your Wings)
23/01/15

I watch you,
as you slowly spread your wings,
and begin to take flight,
I try to follow you,
but my wings aren't strong enough.
Further and further,
you begin to fly away from me,
leaving me on the ground,
running after your shadow,
trying to keep up with you,
calling out your name,
knowing that it's in vain,
that you can't hear my cries,
from that ever increasing height.
You look so beautiful,
soaring through the sky,
oh how I wish I could join you up there,
so we could soar together,
happy at last to have each other.
But here I am, still on the ground,
watching you, with your spread wings,
flying further away from me.

Maybe one day,
you will return to me.
Maybe one day...

Unacknowledged Love
25/01/15

A love that goes unacknowledged,
is the most painful love of all.
Words are left unsaid,
feelings are left unfelt,
and a bitter regret remains,
a wonder of what could have been,
if you had taken the chance,
to have the romance,
you had always wished to have.

Memories of Last Night
30/01/15

It's been so many years,
since you last crossed my mind.
So why did I see you there last night?
Still feel the rapture when I saw you,
even though I knew it was a fantasy.
You re-bewitched my heart,
like you first did, so long ago.

What you did (and still do) to me,
is something that I'm still searching for.
Looking for someone,
who can take my breath away,
without having to do anything,
except be in the same space as me.

I can still feel the intensity of it,
even in my wakened state,
the fantasy still lingers on,
showing no signs of dissipating.

Self-...
30/01/015

Have you ever had a moment,
where all you have running in your mind,
is just a chorus of self-doubt?
Where you find yourself, second guessing yourself,
that nothing you have done,
has not been close to right?

Self-confidence is so fragile,
one day it is right up,
the next it has been shattered down,
and you have that terror,
that lives in the pit of your soul,
steadily growing in a small space of time,
that you've done something wrong,
even though you have no idea, what it is.

And it's at this point,
that you doubt your self-worth,
you're not the best you can be
that they have not seen what it is,
you feel you're best at.
I can remember the last time,
that I felt this way, and I promised myself,
that I would never feel this way again.

But the inevitable has occurred,
and here I am, writing the words,
trying to describe what I feel,
about that internal fear I live with,
every single day, that one day,
nobody will have a use for me.

Opposites Attract
31/01/15

You were hurtful and cruel,
something I guess I was
subconsciously attracted to.
I kept close to you,
trapped by the power you had,
that you never failed to exercise,
leaving me terrified,
yet I'm still in love with you, somehow.

Opposites attract,
some in a good way,
whilst others combust and die;
ours is killing me slowly.
That power I find so irresistible,
keeps drawing me back to you,
putting me back in the Hell,
that people try to take me away from.

I can't explain this feeling,
it's like defusing a bomb,
you keep on going back,
even though it could end you,
that is why I guess they say,
that opposites attract.
There's a passion I feel from you,
that no one else gives to me,
a force that can't be reckoned with.
Even though the emotional bruises don't fade,
new ones continually replacing the old,
I never want to leave you again,
no matter the cost, or the pain.

Secrets And Lies
06/02/15

Sometimes we have to realise that
Everybody has got secrets and lies,
Concealing who they truly are,
Revealing their secrets only when
Everything else has failed,
To keep what they fear most,
Sealed away from prying eyes.

And it is this ever-present fear, which
Never ceases to reassert itself in the mind,
Damaging its host slowly over time.

Life is too short for those secrets,
If only we could be honest with ourselves,
Everything would be so much better,
Shrivelling up the pool of self-hate in the world.

I Swear
08/02/15

I swear to you,
I'll give you all of my love,
all that I am,
just to make you happy.
If I ever make you cry,
then I deserve to be alone,
because if I can't treat you right,
then I deserve to have no one in my life.

I swear to you,
that I'll never let you down.
Be there when you need me,
give you the strength you need,
to fulfil all of your dreams.
All I want in my life,
is just to see you happy.

I swear to you,
that if someone ever causes you hurt,
I will make it go away,
wrap you in a security blanket,
until you feel okay.
I will kiss away your tears,
take away your fears,
I know it sounds cliché,
but I really do mean it.

I swear this to you.

I love you.

10/02/15

I feel like I'm being pulled,
in so many different ways,
till I'm at the point where
I can't think straight.
My will wants to write,
but no words want to be formed,
instead I hear the voice in my head,
telling me to get on with my life.
The same themes going round and round,
no new inspiration left,
everything has ground to a halt,
no more activity inside my brain.
The well of ideas that used to be full,
has dried up and withered away,
don't know if I have anything left to write,
to fill up the rest of my
Little Red Book's pages.

The Dating World
10/02/15

I'm so scared to take this step.
What if I end up getting hurt?
They say you have to take a risk.
Eventually I'll have to enter the dating world.
But it's that fear of the unknown.
Of what could potentially be out there.
Who could be possibly be interested in me?
Will I end up finding someone,
who would want me for me?

Point
17/02/15

There comes a time,
when a point gets pushed
too far, and you wonder why,
I get enraged so fast?
Over and over,
the same point is applied,
somehow you think that,
I'll eventually comply,
but you see that's where you're wrong.
It frustrates me to hear you say,
the same words over and over again,
as if you're trying to prove a point,
that you were right.
And maybe you are,
but that's not the point,
because you don't need to repeat
yourself every few seconds.
I got it the first time,
now we need to move on,
but instead we go in circles,
with you driving your point home.

Be The First
18/02/15

Don't live in the shadow,
of someone who has had success.
Don't try to be "The Next",
because that never really works out.
Be the first of you,
unique in every single way.
Don't conform to what others expect,
don't change who you are,
keep on pressing forward,
keep following your heart.
It's ok to stand out,
and it's ok to be a little different,
I know from personal experience,
that you will be loved for it.

Be the first of you,
don't be the next.
Don't settle for second,
be the best.

State Of Mind
18/02/15

Burnt out;
Phased out;
Nothing matters.

Empty;
Emotionless;
Everything sucks.

Confusion;
Disillusion;
A crisis of self-faith.

Doubts;
Depression;
Mood swings all around.

Desperation;
Fear of rejection;
It is all so very real.

Madness;
Confinement;
This is my state of mind.

18/02/15

Do you know what it's like,
to feel so afraid of what could happen?
When you feel that doubt,
slowly spreading through your body,
causing you to question your self-worth?

Have you ever felt the rollercoaster ride,
where one minute you're riding high,
enjoying the fruits of life,
and then the very next second,
all that euphoria comes crashing down,
ending up back in the well of misery,
that you keep trying to escape?

But that's the thing with depression,
it can hit you so hard, so fast,
you don't even see it coming.
Like a train, it will knock you down,
drag you through the dirt,
hurting you in ways, other people
can't begin to imagine.

You spend so much energy,
trying to build yourself back up again,
and all it takes is a few seconds,
for all your self-confidence,
to be reduced to a rubble,
releasing all that once well contained
self-hate.

Is There Someone Out There?
18/08/15

How long have I been like this?
How could have I been so busy,
not even to notice,
this great weight I'm carrying around,
this feeling of loneliness,
that is gaining ground every day?

I try to explain what I feel to myself,
but the words continually get stuck,
breaking down before they are formed,
so what hope do I have,
if I have to look for professional help?

It's a madness that never ceases,
but I'm trying not to sound like I'm
consistently complaining,
is there someone out there who understands?

My Priorities
18/02/15

Are you proud of me?
Are you proud of what I've achieved?
See, there are the times where I feel,
that what you say is superficial,
because you say one thing,
then follow it up with something else,
that make me doubt your words,
that you didn't mean what you said.

You seem more pleased for me,
when I say something I don't
in real life, really want.

I want a life.
I want to be with someone.
I want to experience a romance.
Those are my priorities,
not everything else.

I Need To Know
18/02/15

What do I have to have to do,
to understand this reality?
What do I have to do,
to make myself see things clearly?
How can I raise the veil,
that has clouded my eyes?

I need to know.
I need to know.

How can I convince my heart,
that ship has sailed for us?
Not a chance in Hell for me to
experience our potential romance.
I still think of the three words,
that you said all those months ago,
replay that moment in my mind,
never letting it fade into memories.
Did you really mean those words?
Or were they said platonically?

I need to know.
I need to know.

But just by an off chance,
that you really meant them,
does that mean there is hope?
Or am I just a stupid fool,
resting all of my hopes on a
hopeless dream?

I need to know.
I need to know.

All these years,
I have been alone.
With no partner in my life,
that I could actually call my own.
No late night cuddles,
no stolen kisses here and there,
I'm back in the slump,
that has broken down,
everything that was repaired.

I need to know.
I need to know.

What does my future hold?
Will I ever find someone?
Or is my fate to only bask
in the remembrance of those two
crushes I once had?
Will they be the only taste I get,
to having feelings for someone?
Is there somebody out there,
strong enough to mend this
broken body and spirit?

I need to know.
I need to know.

Clicked
21/02/15

It amazes me how quickly we clicked,
in only just a few days,
I feel like we've connected in ways
that I never thought possible,
this elated magical feeling.

I don't know how you've done it,
but there's something about you,
that has captured my heart,
and now I can't get enough of you,
we've clicked so fast,
you don't know what you're putting me through.

I would never have thought,
I would have connected so quickly,
to someone I've not met yet,
so strange this is happening,
to me, of all people!

Butterflies
23/02/15

You got me feeling butterflies,
something going on between you and I,
that is so great, but now I'm afraid
that I will mess this up somehow.
We took off so fast, and I'm scared
that we will end up back on the ground,
with all our expectations shattered,
because we didn't share what truly mattered.

I'm so scared that the butterflies I feel,
may never be enough for you.
I want this to work so badly,
and yet the doubts are screaming at me,
that I will never be good enough for you.
You're so good to me, make me so happy,
even though it's been a few days,
it just feels so right when I talk to you.

And that's the other thing that scares me:
what if we suddenly have no words to say?
Just an awkward silence, a void that can't
be filled, and we gradually drift away.
I don't want the butterflies to die,
I want to see if there can be a future
between you and I,
or am I just thinking too much?
Stirring up these thoughts,
scaring me out of my life.

I want to know you so much better,
want to get over the awkward stage,
and I just want there to be comfort,
where we just need each other,
no extra words need to be said.
I'm not much of a talker,
that is the biggest weakness of me,
I feel like I need to say something,
but my insecurities get the best of me,
and no words want to be formed.

I really like you,
and I want something more for us,
and but then there's the part of me,
that wants us to take it slow,
take things step by step,
learn more about each other,
before taking this to the next level.

These butterflies are confusing me,
making me feel so elated and excited,
 they're clouding my judgement,
and I don't know what to think.
This is not because of you,
it all has to do with me and my mind,
I hope I can figure this out in time.

I want you in my life.

01/03/15

Over the past few days,
I guess I've been swept away,
caught up in a moment,
not really thinking straight.
And now I am here,
trying to figure out the thoughts,
that are jumbled in my mind,
wondering what could happen,
if I let this play out over time.

I'm Not The One You Need
02/03/15

Was it all just a fabrication of the mind?
All that I thought and felt,
only existing for a period of time?
I guess the answer I've been wanting,
is finally becoming clearer to me.
That what we could potentially be,
will no more greater than it already is.
And I'm so sorry, I know this is
not what you wished you could hear.
But I know there is someone out there,
who deserves you, who will love you,
and bring you the joy you need.

I'm not the one who can bring you that,
and it would be wrong to mislead you.
Putting up a fake pretence, pretending that
any feelings for you really do exist.
What we had, even though it was brief,
was so great, you can't imagine.
Maybe we can dial it back,
to only just being friends?
I know it would be a lot to ask,
and I wouldn't blame you if you never
spoke to me again.

And if that were to be the case,
I wish you well in your life.
You deserve to be loved by someone
so much better and greater than me.

I'm not the one you need.

A New Hope
02/03/15

I have a new hope instilled in me.
That everything will work out eventually.
All my worries, will be a thing of the past,
finally having what I've wanted most at last.
That all the struggles I have gone through,
are paving the way, leading me to you,
and bringing me to the life I've always wanted,
all the kindness shown to me,
I have never forgotten it.

Everything is going to be ok.
Deep in my heart I know it is.
And on those days that faith wavers,
I know eventually I'll get over it,
moving forward with more determination,
because I know I will make it.

Thoughts From The Author
03/03/15

Thank you for reaching this page! I hope that you have enjoyed what you have read so far.

Even though the book is nearing an end, I thought that now would be a nice time for a little chat.

Whenever I start a new notebook, I always have this fear that one day; I will wake up and realize that I will have nothing more to write about. That the new notebook I have started will remain unfinished and empty.

Although, there is also a sense of excitement, of all the new pieces of writing that I will be noting down, and what the next few months will bring me. I guess that is the innate nature of every writer!

At the time of writing this, I'm looking back through this book, and different poems are bringing back so many different memories. And I look at the remaining blank pages, wondering what will happen to me over the next few weeks. Will it be good? Will I be able to write about it honestly? Will it be relatable to you?

I guess we will have to find out!

W. R. Watkins

Coming Out II
05/03/15

There is never a good time,
to be having this conversation,
just sitting deliberating over
who was going to make the first move.
Who will have the courage to say,
the very words on our minds?

It's time that I come clean to you,
and tell you the truth about us.
I don't think that this can continue,
both of us no longer feel the same.
Whilst we were good for a period of time,
those good times feel like they're over,
and now we're just tolerating what remains.

Breaking up is never easy,
somebody is always hurt.
But you have to do what's best,
especially if you're no longer in love.
You deserve to be with someone,
who will never stop loving you.

Silent Treatment
06/03/15

It's been days since I last spoke to you,
what did I do to deserve this treatment?
I know I said that I could wait,
but I don't know if I have the patience
to endure this silent treatment anymore.

I know you saw my last text,
still have had no reply yet,
do you know how much this hurts me?
I said that I would treat you right,
I said that we could take it slow,
what more do I need to say,
for this silent treatment to end?

It's driving me crazy,
not knowing what's going on in your mind.
When will we be able to move on,
past whatever we're going through?
Please let me know,
don't know what else I can do,
to make this silent treatment finish.

Disconnected Thoughts
06/03/15

I can hear them.

The voices are coming back.

That quiet murmur steadily growing,
now a chorus of screams,
telling me nothing before that was written,
had any truth at all.

All because of one bad comment.
And that's all it takes.
One bad comment negates it all.

All the good you felt about your work,
now has a meaningless to it all.
Was I so deluded by myself,
to think that this could be good work?

How could I have possibly thought,
that I would not get hurt again?

It was bound to happen eventually,
I mean, it's me.

Trying to kid myself,
by saying that it doesn't matter.
All the good comments previously said,
should outweigh this one thing.

But they don't.

Because the negative justifies
that doubt which lingers on,
and validates the fear of rejection,
projecting it further on,
solidifying it in your mind,
to the point where nothing else breaks through.

Springboard
07/03/15

You can beat down on me,
as much as you feel you need,
but you won't break me down.
Not going to let you win again,
I will use this pain to springboard
away from you, break free,
retake the freedom you
stole from me.

And as I walk away from you,
I can feel that strength returning,
rebuilding itself in my soul.
I will never let anyone take it away,
blindly letting them belittle me,
saying that I'm nothing without them,
that I won't amount to much more,
that my dreams are unattainable.

I'm taking all those thoughts,
and gathering them together,
I will use them to springboard away,
propel myself to better things.
Towards something better,
towards the life I feel I was meant to lead.

Repeat After Me
13/03/15

Repeat after me:

"I am indestructible."

"I am not weak."

"I am unbreakable."

"I am not fragile."

"I am invincible."

"I am stronger than you."

"I am undefeatable."

"I am above you."

The Other Side Of Me
14/03/15

Do you know what it feels like,
to have this overflowing rage inside?
To have that other side of you,
threatening to break free?
You have seen what it's capable of,
and it's beyond terrifying,
to think that it could happen again,
unleashed on someone you love.

You just want to hurt everyone,
that is unfortunately in your path,
no matter who benign they are.
This is the side I keep locked away,
only letting a small portion of him out,
when I feel he is needed,
then reigning him back in,
like a rabid dog on a leash,
hoping to scare everyone away,
so that they leave me alone.

On some days, he's easy to control,
tranquilised and tame again,
other days though, he rattles his bars,
screaming to be released,
and like a possessor, taking over me,
and just hurts everyone around him.

It is so blinding,
that he feels nothing else,
except that they deserve his rage,
and all that in entails...

16/03/15

You were the perfect guy,
but at the wrong time.

Did You Think...?
01/04/15

Did you think you had to be there,
each time I opened my eyes,
just to pre-empt a fight?

Did you think you had to support me,
when my self-confidence failed,
telling me everything will be ok?

Did you think I was asking for too much?

Did you think that I set my
expectations so high,
that you felt you had let me down?
Did you think that I had brought
this upon myself,
so now I have to pay the price?

All that I ever wanted from you,
was somebody who would love me,
and somebody whom I could love.
That's all I ever asked for.
Everything else was in your head,
thoughts planted by someone,
who knew you too well.
Driving a stake between us,
creating something that was never there.

I Try
02/04/15

I try to put on a hard exterior,
but it doesn't take much to make me crack.
I put my heart out there,
to get only negativity through back.
No matter how much good you read,
the negative stands out more,
and even though I try to press on,
I get depressed even worse than before.

I try to say "It doesn't bother me",
But in reality it kills me even further,
and all those doubts that I had,
seem justified at long last.
I try to keep the tears from falling,
but I'm slowly failing,
and one-by-one, they steadily fall.

I try to write different lines,
still slowly learning over time,
but it is still not there yet.
I'm not even close to being finished,
I will try and better myself,
until I feel I have written my best.

Shelter
08/04/15

I thought that with you,
at last I had found shelter.
Somebody to stop the storm,
something that would last forever.
But I guess I was fool,
only fooling myself to believe,
that we could be something greater.
All my hopes were in you,
to provide what I wanted,
a physical form of stability,
something other people take for granted.

Phoenix
08/04/15

"...and from the ashes,
like a phoenix, I rise again."

I've been burnt down so many times,
each time I've had to re-build my life,
with a brand new purpose,
only to be knocked back down again.

All my hopes and dreams lie around,
laying on the ground as nothing but ash,
mere remnants of what was to be,
destroyed by those with less belief.

With each misstep I take,
a new lesson is learnt in its wake,
allowing me to move on and
to prove the naysayers wrong.

I gather the ashes, collect the rubble
from the broken house of dreams,
begin to rebuild what it was,
but stronger than what it used to be.

Taller and taller the dreams grow,
making me fight on because I know
that I have got what it takes,
I can survive all the knocks and breaks.

And the next time I am burnt down,
when they think they've won and feeling proud,
like a phoenix, I shall rise once more,
rising from the ashes, once again reborn.

17/04/15

I guess if there's one thing I'm good at,
it's knowing when to walk away.
Close the door, leave the past behind,
because I know that I will be fine.

I don't need you to survive,
I don't need you to succeed.
I wanted you to be a part of it,
to say that you were there for me.

I destroy my connections,
faster than I can build more.
If I feel that I should move on,
I will do it without a second thought.

Some of my plans work out,
others fall to the way-side,
left to be forgotten in time,
how have I left this norm be allowed.

When did I get so closed off,
that now I just ends things so abruptly,
moving on to my next plan,
as if the last meant nothing to me.

"Want" & "Need"
17/04/15

There is a fundamental difference,
between saying you "want" somebody,
compared to saying you "need" somebody.

To say you "want" somebody,
says that you want them as a part of you.
That you want to share your life with them,
share all your insecurities and strengths with them.
You want them to be there when no one else is,
wanting them to see you at your worse,
wanting them to see you at your best.

But if things did not work out,
then you will still live on without them,
the nights will just be more lonely,
and days not filled with the love,
that you once shared together.
But I would survive.
I would be okay without you.
Because I am strong enough to love myself,
enough to carry on living my life.

Now to say you "need" someone,
means that no matter who they are,
you need them to have a purpose.
That if there were to leave you,
you would be moving on,
quickly to the next someone,
to fill that void you cannot bear.

You need that someone,
because you fear fading into oblivion.
You need that someone because,
they will stop the eventual mental-destruction.

It is so much more than just surviving,
it is about needing to feel that affection,
that stops the voice talking about self-termination.

The Memories
19/04/15

I watch you lying there,
so motionless on that hospital bed.
Wires and tubes flowing in
and out of you, fighting
to keep you alive, for just
another month or two.

I sit there at your side,
a solitary tear escapes my eye,
as I hit re-play on the memories,
going over them again in my mind...

...all those talks we had,
talking about everything, they
seemed so silly at the time,
oh how I wish I had cherished them more,
I'd do anything for one last talk.

...how you used to rest your head
against my chest, as we watched
our favourite Disney films,
laughing at the same scenes.
It was perfect.

...the late night walks along the
promenade, hand-in-hand,
gazing up at the stars,
trying to find the brightest one.

Playing in the sand, dodging the waves,
showing off our love, not caring
if others approved or not.

...all those candle-lit dinners,
where we used to stare at each other,
wondering how did we get so lucky,
to have found each other, with
our hands clasped in plain sight.
(I blush at the memory of what we did
later that night).

...the early mornings where, I would
listen to your heart beat, smiling when
you whispered, it was beating for me,
that it was now finally complete.

But now to hear your heart,
there is just a lifeless machine.
The same sound repeated over and over,
I don't feel the comfort that I need,
to know that you're still there with me.
Another machine, they say,
is helping you to still breathe.

...I remember a time, when you said,
that you lost your breath at the
first sight of me,
telling me that I was the most
beautiful person you'd ever seen.

You promised me, that you
would have followed me to the
Ends of the Earth.
You promised me, that you would
never leave me, no matter what
happened between the two of us.
But now, here we are, and I don't know
if I can love ever again.
My heart belongs to you and
nobody else.

I wish that could say the thing,
that I always thought of saying to you.
Can you hear me?
Do you know that I'm still here?
I love you so much,
please don't leave me here alone.
I'm afraid to be alone.

The End.

Final Words from the Author

For a large part of my life, I have kept how I felt and what I thought, to myself. No one really knew what was going on inside my head.

So for me to release a book that is so open and honest, is a big step for me, and if you are reading the Behind The Scenes edition, I have questioned doing this throughout the whole writing process.

However, as I am writing this, there is one quote by the late and great Joan Rivers that is going through my head, and it is the following:

"Tell the truth, it is ok"
- Date Unknown

I'm not perfect. Nobody is. I have my flaws and vulnerabilities. And who doesn't? But they are an important part of me that I cannot forget, because it is those little imperfections that make me who I am. And they make up who you are.

So, if there was one thing that I would like you the reader, to take away from this book, is that it is ok to say that not everything is ok. It is ok to say that everything is not going according to plan. And that it is ok to tell the truth about yourself, and to live the life that will make you happy, not what will make someone else happy.

Be yourself. Love yourself.

Thank you for reading this book.

Acknowledgements

My very first acknowledgements page!

First and foremost, I must say a huge "THANK YOU" to my mum, for reading through this book, the previous one and my very first book, giving me her thoughts and correcting the many (many) errors that inevitably slipped past me (as well as spell checker!). Love you so much!!

Thank you to all of my friends for tolerating my incessant use (and abuse) of my various social media pages! I've said this so many times, and I'm aware that I may sound like a broken record at this point, but I'm so thankful and grateful for you to all still be here, and keeping me in your respective lives. I promised to try and tone down the Social Media use!

A very special thank you, to all the people whom have read, rated and reviewed me previous works. To read such touching reviews, has helped me so much, you have no idea. Sometimes I find myself doubting all the decisions I've made, and that I've made the wrong career choice. But your words continue to encourage and inspire me to continue on writing.

And if you have reached this page, I would like to thank you, the reader, for reading this body of work. I hope you liked at least one poem! I will always thank you, because it is you who allow writers like me to keep on doing what we love and enjoy. I hope I can keep on creating pieces of work that you can enjoy and connect with, for many years to come.

This is only just the beginning for me, and I know I've not created my best work yet.

W. R. Watkins

self-published his first anthology collection *You. Are. Not. Alone.* in July, 2014. The collection contained poetry written from his late teens during Secondary School, focusing mostly upon his own life, as well as exploring romance and teenage angst.

Following the encouragement of the first reviews, he began work on his next book, which would be under the umbrella title of Diary Of The Heart. 'An Obsessive Infatuation', released December 2014, focused upon a one-sided love story, taking the reader through the roller-coaster ride of an infatuation from a distant admirer.

'Little Red Book' soon followed after in August 2015, this time following Watkins' writing process over a year, providing a far more intimate experience for the reader.

He studied 'Animal Behaviour' at Aberystwyth University (Wales), and attended Worth School (Sussex).

Also by W. R. Watkins

You. Are. Not. Alone. (paperback)
You. Are. Not. Alone. (eBook)
You. Are. Not. Alone. (Extended Edition) (paperback)

Diary Of The Heart series:

An Obsessive Infatuation (paperback)
An Obsessive Infatuation (eBook)
An Obsessive Infatuation (Extended Edition) (paperback)

Little Red Book (paperback)
Little Red Book (eBook)
Little Red Book (Behind The Scenes) (paperback)

Lightning Source UK Ltd.
Milton Keynes UK
UKHW04n1334170718
325843UK00001B/25/P

9 781364 497804